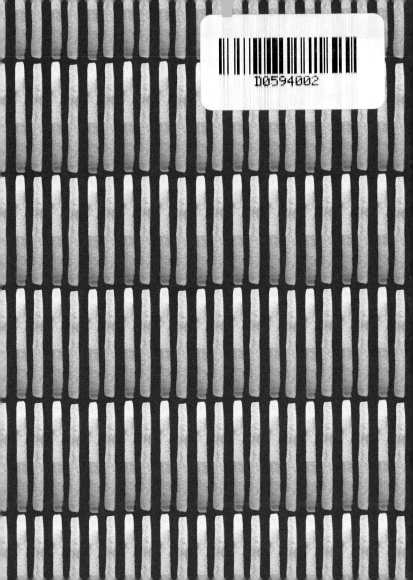

10/17

GONE

FOR

LUNCH

For Annie and Marine, my trailblazers!

Mum and Mim, for never letting me be idle;

And for Steph, for being in need of a letter.

quadrille

GONE FOR LUNCH

52 TH!NGS T✦ DO IN YOUR ⌐UNCH BRE∧K

LAURA ARCHER

INSIDE

OUTSIDE

INTRODUCTION

On a cold and miserably rainy day in January, I made an uncharacteristic move. I decided to take my lunch break.

During a phone call with a friend, a week earlier, I had promised to write her a letter. I had identified several evenings and a weekend afternoon when I could do this, but something always came up; I never seemed to have the time or energy. While joking that there just weren't enough hours in the day, I realized that I actually had almost a full hour of spare time each weekday that I wasn't utilizing: my lunch break.

I had only ever used my lunch breaks for running personal errands or, on the rare occasion that British summertime would occur, at which point I would sit guiltily in the park. Otherwise I would stay working in the office, hunched over my keyboard with a sandwich. But my contract entitled me to a 45-minute break away from my desk every day, so why wasn't I using it?

Part of the reason was that I didn't always know how to spend my break. There are only so many times you can go window shopping, or sit on a park bench, before you start to feel a little despondent. Something always had to call me outside: a friend needed a birthday present, or I needed a new book, or an un-laddered pair of tights. I realized that I had to give myself a reason to get out each day.

I started to draw up a list of things to do. I'm a sucker for a deadline, so I chose to give myself only a week to complete each one, otherwise I knew I would keep delaying it. Thinking I would struggle to come up with more than twelve ideas, I was surprised when I passed the forty mark. Was it really possible to do something different with your lunch break every week of the year?

I then became intrigued to know, out of my list, which was the best way to spend my break. What would be the most exhilarating, or the most relaxing? What would return me to my desk feeling happier, energized and more productive? I also wanted to know how realistic it was to expect to be able to take a full lunch break every day. The next twelve months were there for me to find out.

The results have been surprising. First, I feel as though I've done more in the last year than I had done in the previous five. I have discovered areas of London that I never knew existed, visited exhibitions, learned an unexpected amount of local history, made new friends and had conversations with strangers whose lives have thrown my own into perspective. I have more to think and talk about, and my new-found knowledge of the area around my office has fed directly into my work, allowing me to give a more rounded and informed opinion of current news and trends.

Second, my job satisfaction has sky-rocketed and I have become a much more dedicated employee. As with most 9-to-5ers who dream of a less desk-based life, there was a part of me that hoped I might discover a hidden talent during my reclaimed lunch breaks. I fantasized that, a few months down the line, maybe I'd quit my current role to pursue a devastatingly successful career as an artist, or maybe a gardener.

This was more to do with my state of mind, and body, than any attitude towards my employer. In general, I felt sluggish most days, fairly demotivated and occasionally resentful for being made to sit at my desk until 5.30PM, when I had got through everything I needed to do by 5PM. Everything was grey. I put my lethargy down to the nature of my work: humans are supposed to create, produce, build fires! We are not made to sit at computers.

But what has shocked me is how all those thoughts have evaporated, just from taking a lunch break a couple of times a week. I no longer feel tired and unhealthy, or creatively deprived. It seems that a few twenty-minute, well spent breaks are enough to hit my desire to go and live sustainably in the wild well and truly on the head. I am now thankful for the structure and security of my office job and the company of my colleagues, neither of which I would have as a self-employed freelancer. I get excited about going to work because I associate my working day with exploration and discovery, even though nothing has changed in my role other than the fact that I now approach it with more enthusiasm. Since using my lunch breaks productively, I am satisfied, energetic and when I think of work, it is bright and colourful.

Third, my whole lifestyle has improved. This, I didn't realize until I hit a busy period at work and was unable to take a lunch break for almost three months. I initially noticed how furious I was. Being deprived of a break, after several months of midday freedom, was like being told you can't go to a party you've been looking forward to all year. I felt caged, exasperated and depressed. This initial, violent reaction lasted for about two weeks, after which I accepted my fate and returned to my former grey state of being.

This was when I noticed that my whole life was affected by the lack of a lunch break. The quality of my diet plummeted. By the time I left work each day, I was so low on energy that I would reach for the nearest microwave meal or takeaway menu available. I also drank a lot more alcohol, meeting friends after work with that old familiar line, "God, I need a drink!" or thinking the equivalent to myself when I got home and uncorked a bottle. I rediscovered caffeine, and all the pastries that accompany it. In short, my body was grasping around for energy. The effect knocked on to my weekends too, filled with more drink, more lie-ins, more sugary "treats", and that dreaded Sunday evening feeling that the week is about to begin again. As soon as the busy work period was over, I ran to my lunch breaks as to a friend I hadn't seen in years, and everything else got better.

This book is inviting you to go out for lunch. It is suggesting 52 different things for you to do, as and when you have the time. There is no expectation or demand that you go out every day, or that you need to devote a whole hour to any of the activities. Many of the suggestions that follow only require 20 minutes, once a week, although you can extend this to as long as you want or have.

The activities have been divided up into four sections: **SITTING**, **ACTIVE**, **INSIDE** and **OUTSIDE**. To keep things varied, try to choose an activity from a different section every week, keeping the rhythm regular so that everything alternates reasonably. The minimum amount of time needed is stated at the top of the page, so you can judge what is best for each week, depending on your workload. Some of the activities will require a bit of planning, so you might need to devote your first lunch break of the week to staying at your desk and researching options or routes. By the end of the year, this book should be your own personalized lunchtime resource. There are charts and tables for you to fill in with information about your local area, as well as a space for you to mark how energetic each activity makes you feel.

The focus of the activities is a combination of wellbeing, creativity, relaxation, mindfulness, exploration – and then there are a few that are just a bit fun. The distinction between some of the activities might feel minimal (for example, drawing a portrait versus drawing a building) but they are all there for a reason, as each one will evoke a different response. Some activities will be enjoyed more than others, and some might take more than one go, but never give up and definitely don't give in to eating at your desk if you have the chance to get outside. This is your opportunity to shake off all that tiredness, despondency and frustration with life – and it only takes twenty minutes of your day.

Finally, don't forget: you are being a more efficient employee by taking a lunch break than by not taking one, so never feel guilty for stepping outside.

SITTING

WRITE A LETTER

When did you last sit down and write someone a letter? Not a text, not an email: a proper hand-written letter.

1 Minimum lunch breaks needed

20 Minimum time needed (mins)

LUNCH BREAKS TAKEN

ENERGY OUT OF 10

RATING OUT OF 10

As well as a wonderfully personal way of staying in touch, letters are a brilliant tool for getting your thoughts in order. The fact that you don't receive an instant response from your addressee allows you to really reflect on what you're writing. Edit it, redraft it, consider it.

Find a private, comfortable place to sit, choose your most satisfying notepad and pen and write to:

1. Someone you haven't seen for a long time
2. Your partner
3. Someone you would like to thank
4. Someone who will never receive the letter (an ex, a secret crush, a celebrity or an unrequited love)
5. Yourself... to be opened in five years' time

STUCK FOR INSPIRATION? TRY SOME OF THESE OPENING LINES

I never had the courage to tell you this before, but...

I've been thinking a lot lately about...

I know I text you twenty times a day, and see you every weekend, but I thought I'd just write you a little note to say...

DON'T FORGET
You don't have to send the letter! But make sure you don't leave it lying around in case your secret office crush stops by your desk.

MAKE A LIST OF PEOPLE WHO

Will receive the letter	Will never receive the letter

MEDITATION

Feeling stressed, anxious and just a bit overwhelmed by everything? Try meditating this week to re-focus your attention and achieve some inner calm.

 1 Minimum lunch breaks needed

15 Minimum time needed (mins)

LUNCH BREAKS TAKEN

RATING OUT OF 10

ENERGY OUT OF 10

Studies have shown that, as well as reducing anxiety, meditation actually improves our focus when we're not meditating too, so it's the perfect lunchtime activity for a busy week when you need to be on top of your game – and it only takes 15 minutes.

Alternatively, if you'd rather switch off entirely and have someone else guide you, there are lots of lunchtime meditation classes around. Find your nearest class, or why not ask your employer to set up an in-house session? There are also lots of online tutorials and apps that provide short, structured sessions that you can listen to with headphones.

Find somewhere comfortable and peaceful to sit, close your eyes and practise the following.

DON'T FORGET
To breathe.

1. **Breathing** – breathe in for 4 seconds, hold for 4 seconds, breathe out for 4 seconds. Do this about 10 times to lower heart rate and increase relaxation.

2. **Concentration** – while practising controlled breathing, concentrate on each breath. Focus on the sensation of each breath.

3. **Awareness of body** – now shift your attention to your body, how you are holding yourself, if there is any tension anywhere.

4. **Releasing tension** – relax your shoulders, your back, your neck, your arms and legs.

5. **Clearing your mind** – picture yourself in a cinema, looking at a blank screen. Project all your thoughts onto the screen, your worries, your fears, your hopes and your dreams. There will be spaces between each thought, little gaps of light. Focus on those gaps of light until it blocks out everything on the screen.

6. **Finishing meditation** – slowly become aware of your body again, of the noises and sensations around you. Count down from 15, opening your eyes only when you reach 0.

SITTING

17

DRAW A PORTRAIT*

Unless you're an artist, musician or maker, the majority of your working day is probably filled with words.

LUNCH BREAKS TAKEN

ENERGY
OUT OF 10

1 Minimum lunch breaks needed

15 Minimum time needed (mins)

RATING
OUT OF 10

Emails, letters, phone calls, meetings... they all require you to think and communicate literally. And, as much as we like to pretend that we don't look at our phones during the working day, there are normally a good few text messages flying around too.

Give your brain a break from words – or at least engage another part

of it – by drawing during your lunch break.

If you're not the arty type, this doesn't matter. Drawing is never just about recreating an accurate visual representation of something. Most great artists are appreciated for their style, not their realism. It's about looking, seeing and interpreting. For this challenge in particular, it's about noticing the people around you.

Try a mix of different approaches and see how each produces a different outcome.

- Sit in a park or a café and draw a stranger, or ask a colleague to sit for you.
- Choose a mix of people – old, young, pretty, striking, interesting hair, strange clothes.
- Draw in pen one day, pencil the next, colour felt tip another.
- Limit yourself time-wise for a more sketchy style, or give yourself a full hour for a detailed masterpiece.

DON'T FORGET
If you're drawing an un-knowing stranger, make sure they're not three-quarters of their way through a sandwich when you start, or you won't have very long to study them...

* There are a few different drawing challenges in this book. If you want something more modular, which still requires looking but involves a fair amount of "filling in", turn to page 112 for **DRAW A BUILDING**. If you want to switch off entirely, focusing only on the page without having to look up and almost going into a trance-like state, turn to page 26 for **DOODLE**.

WRITE OR READ A POEM

It's not beyond the bounds of possibility that you haven't written a poem since school – apart from that one you wrote to an ex a couple of years ago, which you tore up immediately afterwards, or just hid very well.

1 Minimum lunch breaks needed

45 Minimum time needed (mins)

LUNCH BREAKS TAKEN

RATING OUT OF 10

ENERGY OUT OF 10

Poetry doesn't have to be grand or over-bearing, reserved only for weddings and funerals, love and heartbreak. Think of writing a poem as similar to taking a photo, although instead of capturing an image you are capturing a sensation – and this could be of something as mundane as looking out of your window.

If you need some help, one of the best guides about writing poetry is a book called *Poetry in the Making* by Ted Hughes. Hughes insists that any form of creative writing is not about "how to write" but "how to say what you really mean". So forget about rhyming, rhythms and sounding like Shakespeare. This week is about considering how you respond to something and getting the words down on paper.

Whether reading or writing it this week, poetry is a brilliant form of therapy. First, it's all about you: your response, your emotions, your interpretation, your vocabulary. Which, in the middle of a working day, when you've spent the whole morning touting your company's party line, should feel refreshing and restorative.

Second, through articulating your feelings and experiences, you will be making sense of them and gaining a better understanding of your mood in certain types of situation.

For inspiration – or reassurance – spend a couple of lunch breaks reading poems before you start writing your own. Browse through a few poetry anthologies in your local bookshop or visit the Poetry Foundation's website, which has almost every poem ever written freely available to read and organized by theme, so it's easy to navigate.

SOME TOPICS TO GET YOU STARTED

- **The view from your office window** – what does it make you wonder about?

- **A nearby tree** – how has the city changed around it as it's grown?

- **Your happiest moment ever**.

- **Someone you haven't seen for a while** – what do you remember most about them?

READ A BOOK YOU'VE ALWAYS MEANT TO*

We've all got them... Those books that, with every good intention, we've promised ourselves we'll read on our next holiday. Then you reach the airport, sidle into the magazine-cum-bookshop in the departures lounge and come out with 3-for-2 trashy novels.

5 Minimum lunch breaks needed

30 Minimum time needed (mins)

LUNCH BREAKS TAKEN

RATING OUT OF 10

ENERGY OUT OF 10

Make this the week you actually tackle the beast and set aside your lunch breaks to get into a book that you've been dying to read for years, but just haven't had the time or energy for.

Although it states that five lunch breaks of at least half an hour are needed, that's only if you want to finish the whole book using only your lunch breaks. Reading is actually one of the most flexible lunchtime challenges in this book. Where other activities require planning, good weather or a fixed location, book reading will fit around any restriction you throw at it. And even on days when the thought of leaving your emails unattended makes you break out in a cold sweat, you can just shift the book reading to your commute.

Whether for 5 minutes or 50, the smallest amount of time spent reading will still provide your mind with a doorway out of the office and a refreshing dip into a parallel universe.

Find a cosy, quiet spot, or a refreshingly open one, and allow yourself to become absorbed.

* If you haven't got a book in mind, do the **BOOKSHOP BROWSING** challenge on page 84 first.

DON'T FORGET
This is supposed to be fun! If you're not enjoying it, you're probably not reading the right book. If this is the case, cast it aside in favour of something better.

BOOKS YOU READ THIS WEEK

LUNCH WITH FRIENDS

You see them so often, and share everything with each other, that it's easy to think you know your friends inside out.

1 Minimum lunch breaks needed

45 Minimum time needed (mins)

LUNCH BREAKS TAKEN

ENERGY OUT OF 10

RATING OUT OF 10

But often it can be this exact level of intimacy that prevents us from seeing the bigger picture when it comes to our friends' hopes, fears and ambitions. As your closest confidants, friends can quickly turn into agony aunts or counsellors: you will spend half an hour together deconstructing a particular glance someone threw you, or diagnosing why a certain comment sent you into a tailspin.

While all of this is part of the joy of being friends, you can get a bit bogged down in the emotional and psychological detail. Keep things light and broad this week and focus on the long-term future, rather than the immediate past.

Avoid talking about things that annoy or upset you and instead discuss who or what inspires you. Ask each other where you'd like to be in five years' time: professionally, romantically and/or geographically. Plan a fantasy holiday together, or dream up a business idea. Keep it as positive, creative and future-oriented as possible.

If you don't work near any of your close friends, extend this to include people who you aren't in your immediate circle, but who work near you. Even if they're not friends at the beginning of the week, they might well be by the end of it – and it never hurts to get to know someone new.

DON'T FORGET
Avoid moaning, gossiping and talking about exes.

You met	You went to	You talked about

DOODLE

This is ideal for when you're not able to take a lunch break at all, especially if you're stuck in a meeting or on a call.

LUNCH BREAKS TAKEN

ENERGY
OUT OF 10

RATING
OUT OF 10

1 Minimum lunch breaks needed

15 Minimum time needed (mins)

Doodling is often associated with wasting time or not really paying attention (and therefore, in theory, perfect for a lazy lunch break when you want to feel close to unconscious!).

However, studies have shown that doodling actually heightens our concentration and puts us in what's been called a "perfect state of listening". We are able to hear everything that is being said but, because we are simultaneously focusing on the doodles in front of us, our mind is unable to wander.

At the same time, doodling gives our brain some down-time and allows us to relax a little, providing us with a break, even if we've been sitting in the same meeting room all day. It is also rumoured to heighten creativity, as it stops you from thinking at a million miles an hour, focuses your attention and lets the cogs keep turning subconsciously. So you might find that, after a good doodle, the solution to a problem you've been chewing over all day suddenly appears.

All this being said, you don't need to be stuck in the office to doodle. Take it outside with you and zone out for anything from 15 minutes to a full lunch break, if you've got enough doodle in you.

DON'T FORGET
It's not a work of art! A doodle can be anything, from names or signatures repeated over and over again to cartoons to abstract patterns and scribbles.

DOODLE ALL OVER THIS PAGE

LISTEN TO AN ENTIRE BALLET OR OPERA

Whatever music genre we prefer, we usually listen to our favourite songs or movements on repeat.

5 Minimum lunch breaks needed

30 Minimum time needed (mins)

LUNCH BREAKS TAKEN

RATING OUT OF 10

ENERGY OUT OF 10

We use music as a way to enhance our own mood, to pick us up or keep us motivated, or to provide some discreet noise in the background, to obscure the silence.

Rarely do we turn to music to learn something. The scores written for operas and ballets are not just music; they are a means of communicating a story, even a lesson. They are tales of love, loyalty, human struggle, tragedy, disaster, remorse and redemption. They can challenge the strength of our convictions, or put our own personal dilemmas into perspective.

Acquire some new knowledge in a different way this week and listen to an entire opera or ballet over the course of several lunch breaks.

There are a few suggestions below, if you need a bit of help selecting something to listen to. Whatever you choose, read a brief synopsis of the plot before you put your headphones on, so that you have a vague understanding of what is happening at each point. This isn't cheating; in fact you'd be an uninformed opera or ballet goer if you didn't know the story in the first place.

BALLETS ABOUT...

- The fight between good and evil: *Swan Lake*, Tchaikovsky
- Love and the stupidity of holding grudges: *Romeo and Juliet*, Prokofiev
- Deception and heartbreak: *Giselle*, Adolphe Adam

OPERAS ABOUT...

- Unrequited love and not appreciating what's in front of you: *Eugene Onegin*, Tchaikovsky
- The battle of the sexes: *The Marriage of Figaro*, Mozart
- Trying – and tragically failing – to outwit the authorities: *Tosca*, Puccini

SOMETHING A LITTLE MORE MODERN...

- *Porgy and Bess*, Gershwin
- *Les Parapluies de Cherbourg*, Jacques Demy

DON'T FORGET

The musical style of each ballet or opera will vary so greatly. If you aren't getting on with your first choice, try another one until something clicks.

WRITE A NOVELETTE

Apparently we've all got one book in us, one story that's as unique as our genetic makeup and has the potential to be the world's next bestselling novel.

 5 Minimum lunch breaks needed

45 Minimum time needed (mins)

 LUNCH BREAKS TAKEN

 RATING OUT OF 10

ENERGY OUT OF 10

Unfortunately, very few of us have the time to extract, note down and edit the full 40,000 words that it takes to qualify as a novel but, at only 7,500 words, you might be able to manage a novelette during lunch this week.

Spread over 5 days, you will need to write 1,500 words (roughly three typed or six handwritten pages of A4) a day. Of course, if you're really

aiming to get this done in week, you can use evenings and weekends too.

At this amount and speed, you're not looking to make every sentence perfect. It's about the experience of developing a plot and writing something longer than a short story. Don't be intimidated by the idea that you're writing a small novel: make it lighthearted or trashy if that helps take the pressure off and, most of all, just enjoy having the chance to tell your colleagues that, sorry, you can't join them for lunch today; you're "working on your novelette".

SOME TIPS FOR GETTING STARTED

- **Plan** – start by choosing what genre your novelette will fit into: horror, romance, comedy, tragedy, etc. Then plan the plot – choose the characters, the setting, the conflict, the climax. Remember that you haven't got a lot of words, so don't make it too complex. Discuss your ideas with friends and family (maybe use the weekend before to do the planning). This will help develop the plot and iron out any inconsistencies.

- **Always keep the central idea in focus** – you haven't got time or space to wander off exploring sub-plots. Don't lose sight of the main story: keep it tight. If you have several threads to the plot, consider breaking the novelette up into sections, although probably no more than three.

DON'T FORGET
This is an intensive challenge; it needs to be done during a very quiet week.

Continued...

- **Set up a conflict** – most stories revolve around some form of conflict, with two worlds colliding. Consider what yours will be – boy vs. girl, old vs. young, society vs. nature, fantasy vs. reality, person vs. themselves, etc.

- **Foreshadow** – the beginning of your novelette doesn't need to be the start of the story. Giving your readers a momentary glimpse of the future is a great way of instantly creating suspense and intrigue.

- **Show, don't tell** – rather than telling your reader, "It was a cold morning when Mark left home..." show them by saying "Mark could see his breath as he stepped outside, the sun still low in the sky..."

PLAN YOUR NOVELETTE HERE

LEARN A LANGUAGE

This is a great challenge to do the week before you set off on holiday!

5 Minimum lunch breaks needed

30 Minimum time needed (mins)

LUNCH BREAKS TAKEN

RATING OUT OF 10

ENERGY OUT OF 10

Learning a new language can feel like a mammoth task, especially when you think back to school and the hours you spent trying to remember French verbs – and you can still only just about order two croissants in a boulangerie. The good news is, though, that you don't need to learn a lot to be able to have a basic conversation. In French, for example, only 600 words account for 90%

of words found in common text (newspapers, blogs etc.).

Don't feel burdened by this task; try to make it enjoyable. Learning from books, like you did at school, is not the only way to go. Consider some of the options below; try a couple of them out on your first lunch break and push ahead with the most accessible one for the rest of the week.

DIFFERENT WAYS TO LEARN A NEW LANGUAGE

Audio guide or podcast – if the thought of getting a notebook out and writing everything down fills you with dread, audio guides and podcasts feel a lot less cumbersome because all you need is a pair of headphones. There are so many out there – some free and some not. Although not free, Michel Thomas is one of the easiest, most effective and empowering audio guides around. Available to download worldwide, you can begin with his Foundation course, which doesn't cost too much and only requires 1.5 hours of listening. You'll be surprised how much you can say after just 15 minutes (not just, "Hello. How are you? What's your favourite colour?").

Apps – if you prefer to be more interactive in the way you learn, and enjoy point-scoring and rewards, apps are the most engaging option. Type the language that you'd like to learn into the search bar of your app store and have a look through the results – there will be lots of different formats and levels to suit your style of learning. Even if you decide to learn primarily via headphones or textbook, apps can also be a great supplementary learning tool, to test your knowledge or vocabulary at the end of the day.

Continued...

DON'T FORGET
To stop when your brain feels tired. There's no exam at the end of this.

Textbooks – if you prefer to see everything laid out on a page, so that you can jump back and forwards between what you're learning, the traditional, paper-based route might be the one for you. As the most visual way of communicating information, the formatting of a textbook can either make or break your learning. With this in mind, try to spend your first lunch break browsing through the various textbook options in your nearest bookshop, or if you aren't near one and need to order online, make sure you read the reviews of each book you're considering.

Conversation – if you learn more from hearing other people speak, and being regularly corrected, you might be better off seeking out some company and learning with another person – or a group of people. For the first option, you could ask a foreign colleague if they wouldn't mind meeting you for lunch every other day and teaching you. Alternatively, search online for any ads from people offering conversation time. It doesn't even have to include meeting up – a lot of people offer phone or video-call conversation classes. If you're more of a group learner, search online for language conversation groups near your office. Community-based websites are always good for these and if you don't find anything, you could always create a group of your own and see if anyone else nearby has the same idea.

WRITE A NEW SENTENCE
YOU HAVE LEARNED EACH DAY

What I learned	What it means

READ A NEWSPAPER

With so much news so easily accessible online, it's no great surprise that the number of people who buy and read printed newspapers is on the decline.

LUNCH BREAKS TAKEN

ENERGY
OUT OF 10

1 Minimum lunch breaks needed

30 Minimum time needed (mins)

RATING
OUT OF 10

Comprehensive and considered as the printed versions may be, we have often already seen or heard about most of the stories online by the time they go to print.

But think about the way you use an online news site compared to how you read a newspaper. Even if you begin by logging on to a specific website to read the daily news and begin with the most recent post, you'll soon be distracted by a link to another article, written maybe months ago, that is somehow connected to the story you just read. Once you've clicked on that link, you'll be directed to another loosely related item. Suddenly you're no longer reading the latest news, but building up a small, mental portfolio of stories that all have roughly the same message.

This isn't bad – if anything you are becoming informed about a specific topic – but, from a day-to-day perspective, it can mean we get slightly obsessed, panicked or harangued by a single point of view.

Newspapers, by the very nature of their bookish appearance, encourage you to move from start to finish. A mixture of stories on each page means that, even if a particular item doesn't interest you, you'll probably still read everything. And by going through all the pages, you'll also be carried through each section: world news, local news, arts and culture, sport,

opinion and review. You come away having had a much more rounded, and consequently calmer, experience.

Try to read a different newspaper each day, so that you can get a sense of the different points of view and reporting styles of each one.

DON'T FORGET
You don't have to read every section, but try to be as broad as possible.

PLAY A GAME OF CHESS (OR ANY OTHER BOARD GAME)

Chess is one of those magical games that tick all the right boxes.

1 Minimum lunch breaks needed

40 Minimum time needed (mins)

LUNCH BREAKS TAKEN

RATING OUT OF 10

ENERGY OUT OF 10

Extensive research has shown how playing chess raises your IQ, improves your memory and concentration, increases creativity (by engaging both sides of the brain), develops your problem-solving skills, and teaches planning and foresight. All of which are probably key points that appear under the "personal qualities" section of your job description.

On top of this, playing chess also helps prevent Alzheimer's disease and, through requiring focus and reflection, lowers blood pressure and reduces stress levels (unless you're losing). There's also the social and relationship-building side of the game – while it's possible to play on your own, most of the time chess requires a partner.

Ask around in the office and see if there are any colleagues who know how to play and who would enjoy a brief lunchtime game. If you've never played chess before, don't try to teach yourself from books or online manuals. The best way to learn chess is by playing, so ask a colleague to teach you.

If there's absolutely no one around to play chess with, try another game – backgammon, Scrabble, word and number games, or card games. Choose something that will challenge your brain slightly, and get you thinking and strategizing.

DON'T FORGET
To protect your king.

If you enjoy this and quickly notice the mental benefits of playing, you could ask your employer to set up a chess or board game tournament in the office. Playing against colleagues encourages cooperation, develops understanding of each other and helps you learn how to interact when one of you is in the losing position.

Don't get too serious about winning though; you could end up reversing all these great benefits!

KNIT A SCARF

If you're craving a cosy, creative way to spend your lunch break this week, it might be time to get your knitting needles out.

 5 Minimum lunch breaks needed

45 Minimum time needed (mins)

 LUNCH BREAKS TAKEN

RATING OUT OF 10

 ENERGY OUT OF 10

Knitting is a craft that can be as complex as you want it to be. If you've never knitted before in your life, a straightforward scarf is the perfect place to start.

There are lots of different varieties of knitting needle. For a scarf, you will need a pair of long, straight needles. Since you only have a week to make the scarf, select a pair of needles with a fairly thick diameter: the thicker the needle, the larger the stitch (and therefore the fewer stitches needed). Likewise, choose a thick yarn so that fewer stitches – and less time – are required. Ask for advice from the shop assistant when choosing your knitting needles and yarn, as certain yarns work best with certain knitting needles, so you want to make sure you choose the right ones.

Find an online tutorial to show you how to get started. Make sure you use the search term "how to knit a scarf for beginners" so that you are taken through the basics step-by-step. There are two main stitches for knitting a straight scarf – "plain" and "pearl". Although you can get away with using only plain stitch, this will mean that the scarf looks different on each side, whereas if you use both stitches, the scarf will look the same whichever way round.

Knitting is shown to have so many health benefits, from increased concentration and focus, lowering blood pressure and heart rate, to reducing feelings of stress, anxiety and depression. On top of all this, you'll end the week with something comfy to wear, snuggle into or give away, not to mention a glowing sense of pride as you parade your new creation in front of your envious colleagues.

DON'T FORGET
To keep the yarn loose. If it gets too tight the whole process becomes stressful.

SET SOME GOALS

Where do you want to be in five years' time? Do you dream of a different life, perhaps moving to a different city or country, or are you pretty satisfied with your current lot and just hope that the roots you've put down will keep growing?

1 Minimum lunch breaks needed

30 Minimum time needed (mins)

LUNCH BREAKS TAKEN

ENERGY OUT OF 10

RATING OUT OF 10

Whether you have big dreams or little ones, it never hurts to take some time to stop, think about them and set yourself a deadline. Begin by making a list of your dreams. How are you going to get to where you want to be? And how soon do you need to start moving in order to get there on time?

Perhaps you want to take a year off work to go travelling: how will you fund this and when do you need to start saving? What do you need to do to make sure you'll be able to get a good job when you return? Could you get some experience while abroad, or is there something you could add to your résumé now that will put you in a stronger position when you come back?

Or do you love your job but feel it's time for a promotion, or hope that one will come your way in a couple of years? Invite your manager out for lunch and ask them what sort of opportunities there are for you within the company. Don't demand; just let them know of your dedication, interest and optimism for the future.

Or maybe your dreams are more creative: you'd like to write a book, or develop an artistic or musical talent. Look into courses you could enroll on or, if you know anyone who is creatively where you want to be, spend your lunch break with them one day and ask them how they got there. If they don't live or work near you, schedule a call.

Whatever you intend to do with your life, make sure you write it all down now and keep it in a safe and memorable place. You'll be surprised by how much has actually come true when you dig it out a few years later.

DON'T FORGET
To dream big.

Goal	Timeframe	What you need to do

LOCAL MARKETS

Think of a market and you will probably think of colour, activity, variety, noise, smells, flavours...

LUNCH BREAKS TAKEN

ENERGY OUT OF 10

1 Minimum lunch breaks needed

25 Minimum time needed (mins) + journey time

RATING OUT OF 10

Now think of your usual lunchtime: how many of those words apply? Use your lunch breaks this week to add a bit of welcome chaos to your day and visit your nearest market.

Not only should this excite your senses and break up the monotony of your usual routine; markets are great places to broaden

your horizons. If you're feeling chatty, strike up some conversations with stallholders, see where they've come from and how long they've been trading.

If you're based in a location where there aren't any nearby markets, you could try vintage, antique or charity shops for variety.

If it's craftsmanship you're after, see if there are any studios or workshops near you.

DON'T FORGET
Your wallet.
Impossible not
to get tempted.

FIND YOUR NEAREST MARKET

Market	When	What you bought/tasted

GO FOR A RUN

If you're feeling sluggish, tired and demotivated, it could be time to lace up, hit the pavements and get the blood flowing with a good run during lunch this week.

 1 Minimum lunch breaks needed

5 Minimum time needed (mins) + changing time

 LUNCH BREAKS TAKEN

RATING OUT OF 10

 ENERGY OUT OF 10

While this might feel like the last thing you want to do right now, studies have shown that going for a run for just 5 minutes a day improves your brain performance, your mood and the quality of your sleep. On a more long-term health basis, too, running also reduces high blood pressure and cardiovascular disease and, in general, can increase life expectancy by an extra three years.

If you're not a regular runner and the thought of running solo through the streets around your office feels awkward, lunchtime running clubs are a big thing in most cities. Search online for your nearest club or, if there isn't one, you could always set one up with some colleagues.

Don't force yourself, though. If running really isn't for you, 15 minutes brisk walking a day will apparently also do the trick. Alternatively, go for a short run nearer home one morning or evening, before you start this challenge. This will give you a sense of your pace, your limits, and how long you need to cool off afterwards!

However long you choose to run for, always make sure you:

- Warm up and warm down – there's nothing worse than returning from lunch with a torn hamstring.

DON'T FORGET
To check that your workplace has a working shower before you head off.

- Keep your arms at right angles and to the sides of your body, i.e. don't let them cross over your torso as you're running, as this restricts breathing and makes running much harder.

- BREATHE! Not just normally, without thinking about it. Really consider the rhythm and intensity of each breath. If it helps, count to four each time you breathe in and out. Air is your fuel, so keep your body properly topped up throughout the run.

YOUR PERSONAL BEST THIS WEEK

Distance:

Time:

BIKE RIDES

If you're really wanting to put some physical distance between you and the office, meet your new, closest ally: the bicycle.

1 Minimum lunch breaks needed

45 Minimum time needed (mins)

LUNCH BREAKS TAKEN

ENERGY OUT OF 10

RATING OUT OF 10

Taxis and public transport aside, a bike will take you places your legs just can't carry you in a lunch break.

Use this freedom wisely. Think about all the places you would love to spend your lunch, but are just too far the rest of the time. Go online and look at a map of the areas adjoining your usual stomping ground. Find somewhere or something interesting and get peddling.

The average cycling speed is around 15km or 9 miles an hour. With this in mind, aim for somewhere about 3.5km or 2 miles away. This is a healthy distance, which you can easily cover in less than 15 minutes, while still allowing a good

15–20 minutes to stop for lunch when you get there. The sense of being literally miles away from the office will also make your heart skip – in a good way.

Many cities have rent-a-bike schemes, with docking stations based every half mile or so. If you don't have one of these near you, look into renting from a bike hire shop, or take your own bike with you and cycle into work this week.

If you're not used to biking around big cities, make sure you follow these safety tips.

BICYCLING SAFETY TIPS

- Wear a helmet.
- Always look both ways.
- Indicate with your arms when turning.

DON'T FORGET
Pedestrians can't always hear you coming and often won't look both ways before crossing a road, especially if there's no traffic around. Make sure you have a bell, or a loud voice, at the ready.

- Stick to the side-streets if possible.
- Don't cycle too close to the curb – this makes cars think they have more space to overtake you than they do.
- Ride a door's width from a car, especially if they are stationary or parked.
- Always stop at red lights – it's tempting to go straight through, but it's illegal and you can get fined. It's also much safer to wait.

LISTEN TO A PODCAST

It's nice to be entertained – especially when you can press "pause" if you need to rush back to the office.

| 1 | Minimum lunch breaks needed |
| 30 | Minimum time needed (mins) |

LUNCH BREAKS TAKEN

ENERGY
OUT OF 10

RATING
OUT OF 10

Sometimes you need a bit of distraction from your own thoughts, but going for lunch with a friend or colleague just doesn't grab you (you'll only end up talking about the things you need distracting from). Neither do you want to spend your lunch break in silence, though, even if you are doodling, wandering or sitting in a park.

Podcasts can provide the perfect type of company in situations like these. With so many genres and topics to choose from – comedy, documentary, history, sports, crime, etc. – you are presented with just the right-sized portion, and the right type, of engaging conversation.

Search online for the "top ten podcasts" and see if any of the ones listed take your fancy. Look for this list on an online news site or blog, rather than a techy or a chart listings site, as you will get a much more personal review of each podcast and a description of what each one is about.

Combine your listening with a walk around your local area – this is a good way of measuring time and getting some gentle exercise into your lunch break as well.

DON'T FORGET
You don't have to listen to the whole podcast in one go. A full 30 or 60 minutes of another person's voice can sometimes be a bit much, so start with 15 minutes and see how you go.

PODCASTS YOU HAVE LISTENED TO THIS WEEK

GALLERIES/MUSEUMS

If you work in a big city, you are probably lucky to be surrounded by several galleries or museums that tourists from around the globe flock to – but when was the last time you visited an exhibition there?

LUNCH BREAKS TAKEN

ENERGY OUT OF 10

RATING OUT OF 10

1 Minimum lunch breaks needed

45 Minimum time needed (mins) + journey time

If you don't live near a major cultural institution, consider commercial galleries, auction houses, churches, libraries and town halls: all of these will have some fascinating and beautiful works of art and craftsmanship in their collections.

If you're not a regular visitor of galleries or museums and find them slightly overwhelming, worrying that you don't know enough about what you're looking at, or finding yourself easily bored and feeling guilty about it, fear not!

Approach the gallery or museum in the same way that you would a bookshop. When you enter a bookshop, you are never expected to look at every book on the shelves. You pick one out that catches your eye and give it time and attention, getting to know and understand it better. If the bookshop analogy doesn't grab you, liken it to clothes shopping: when did you ever try on all the clothes in a shop?

A gallery or museum is exactly the same. Walk around a bit, briefly scanning the objects as you go and only stop to look at something when your body actually physically stops, without you making it. Then go up to the object, study it, ask yourself why it made you stop, read about it if there is an information label next to it, and take a picture (if you're allowed to). At the end of the week, look back through the photos of the objects you loved and see if there are any trends – a common colour, shape, style or subject matter. You will learn a lot about your taste and it will make you a more confident exhibition-goer in future.

DON'T FORGET
If only one object makes you halt in your tracks, that's fine. It's much better to look at one object intently than several objects disinterestedly.

CLIMB TO THE HIGHEST POINT

Viewing cities from high up is always fun. It feels invigorating, it gives us a sense of our bearings and it often surprises us to discover how much closer everything is.

 1 Minimum lunch breaks needed

 15 Minimum time needed (mins) + journey time

 LUNCH BREAKS TAKEN

RATING OUT OF 10

 ENERGY OUT OF 10

In short, it makes us feel much more connected to a city and gives us a greater sense of control when navigating our way around.

And while there's no research to prove that being high in the sky is beneficial for your mind or body, the fresh air and sense of limitlessness certainly can't be a bad thing.

Find your nearest café or bar at the top of a skyscraper, viewing platform, church spire or tower this week and don't stop until you reach the top! When you get there, it's up to you if you just want to admire the view, spend your time landmark-spotting, take a panoramic photo or get your sketchpad out and trace the skyline.

DON'T FORGET
If the building you're aiming for doesn't have a lift, be prepared for a rather strenuous climb and be realistic about how long it will take you to get to the top, so that you can be back at work in good time. You don't want to have to rush all the way down to the bottom again as soon as you've got there.

DRAW THE HIGHEST BUILDING THAT YOU CLIMBED TO THE TOP OF HERE

ARCHITECTURE

Architecture – both civic and religious – is where we, as humans, put all our effort and devotion.

1 Minimum lunch breaks needed

20 Minimum time needed (mins) + journey time

LUNCH BREAKS TAKEN

RATING OUT OF 10

ENERGY OUT OF 10

The buildings we design represent and incorporate our aspirations and joys, as well as our fears and losses. They are also works of art, feats of engineering and important places of public gathering.

Visit a few different types of buildings this week and think about the messages they convey, the values they uphold and the welcome they extend (or maybe don't extend). What do they tell you about your own society, or about a religion? Is the atmosphere peaceful, intimidating or awe-inspiring?

These buildings could include government buildings, town halls, churches, synagogues, mosques, libraries, art galleries, museums, etc. They could be centuries old or very recent constructions – you could even include buildings that haven't yet been built! Don't spend time thinking about what is inside the building, in terms of content. Focus purely on the architecture, the exterior and interior elevations, the space the building occupies and how it makes use of it.

If you're in a location where there are several of one type of building (e.g. churches or museums), visit a few and compare how each one presents itself differently. Maybe they were built in different historical eras; what does the development of the architectural style tell you about how thinking changed over the years?

Take photographs, make sketches, and write down notes about each building (if desired). By the end of the week you will have a much richer sense of the temperaments and beliefs of the people who have lived in your local area over the centuries.

DON'T FORGET
To look up.

BUILDINGS YOU HAVE VISITED THIS WEEK

EXERCISE (NOT RUNNING)

If **GO FOR A RUN** (page 50) isn't quite your idea of mentally engaging exercise – in fact, even if it is – think about alternative forms of exercise this week.

1 Minimum lunch breaks needed

30 Minimum time needed (mins) + journey time

LUNCH BREAKS TAKEN

ENERGY OUT OF 10

RATING OUT OF 10

This could be yoga, swimming, playing tennis, football, basketball, going to the gym, signing up for a dance or aerobics session... anything you enjoy and that can fit into half an hour, so that you still have time to get back to work and have a quick shower. If you have the right resources, try a different form of exercise each day and see how each one makes you feel afterwards.

If the form of exercise you've chosen is a team sport – for example football or tennis – ask a few colleagues if they'd like to join you. The act of playing together will improve communication skills, strengthen team bonds and in general help to forge relationships.

It will also relieve any tension that you might have built up in working together, especially if you've just completed a stressful project.

If you're engaging in a team sport, make sure you have a bit of leeway time-wise for getting back, so you can enjoy reliving the highlights afterwards, rather than all rushing back to your desks.

DON'T FORGET
To check for that all-important work shower (again).

Type of exercise	Time spent exercising	Notes (e.g. scores, team-mates)

COMMERCIAL ART GALLERIES

Although this might seem similar to the **GALLERIES/MUSEUMS** challenge (page 56), commercial galleries allow you to interact with art in a very different way.

LUNCH
BREAKS
TAKEN

ENERGY
OUT OF 10

RATING
OUT OF 10

1 Minimum lunch breaks needed

30 Minimum time needed (mins)

Commercial art galleries can be intimidating places. They are often exposed, fairly empty, white cubes with just a gallery assistant sitting behind a desk. There's a sense that only collectors can enter, but this isn't the case. Most commercial art galleries — especially contemporary ones — have put a lot of time and thought into curating their exhibitions. They are working to promote artists and to help them become better known, so the more people who go to view the exhibition, the better, even if you can't afford to buy anything.

The gallery staff will also be very willing to talk to you. While in public galleries and museums, the staff are there to invigilate – making sure you don't step over the invisible line surrounding an artwork – commercial gallery staff are there to sell. They will be informed about the works on show (perhaps they have worked directly with the artist); and as there are very few visitors to commercial galleries, they will have the time to share their knowledge and discuss the pieces with you. Even better: sometimes they might even let you pick up the work of art, look at its back or its underneath.

Finally, while the purpose of a public gallery is to establish a history of art, displaying a linear progression of artistic development, commercial galleries can be much more diverse, experimental and controversial in the stories they choose to communicate. Find your nearest ones and enjoy a more open approach to viewing art.

DON'T FORGET
Don't be afraid to talk and ask questions – the gallery assistant has probably been waiting to speak to someone all day!

DESK YOGA

On days when it just isn't possible to step away from your desk, you can still give yourself a break and a boost with a few desk-based yoga exercises. Originating in India, yoga is a millennia-old system of physical, mental and spiritual practices that all aim to connect the body and mind, or soul. Literally translated, "yoga" means "connection" or "union".

 1 Minimum lunch breaks needed

 10 Minimum time needed (mins)

 LUNCH BREAKS TAKEN

 RATING OUT OF 10

 ENERGY OUT OF 10

Applying the belief that "you are how you feel" to the workplace, if your body is feeling sluggish, it's likely that your mind is sluggish too. Wake yourself up physically and you'll also achieve mental revitalization.

All of the exercises below are relatively low-key – no yoga mats required – and they have been listed according to levels of discretion so your colleagues don't even need to know what you're doing, although try to do at least three or four exercises to get the maximum benefit.

Warm up – before practising any of the exercises below, edge forward to the front of your seat and make sure your feet are both firmly on the ground. Take a deep breath in and then exhale slowly. Drop your chin to your chest, then look up to the ceiling. Repeat this several times, a bit like a nod. Next, look alternately to the left and right, first without dropping your head, then rolling your chin on your

chest, like a U-shape from shoulder to shoulder. Finally, roll your shoulders back several times, then forward several times. Finish with another deep inhale and exhale.

DISCREET

Backbend – seated with a straight spine, take a deep breath in and reach all the way up to the ceiling with your arms open wide. As you exhale, slowly look up to the ceiling, bending slightly backwards from your upper back and chest. Hold this for a few seconds, release arms to your sides, then repeat a few times. Combine this with a large yawn for ultimate discretion!

Twist – sit in your chair with your spine tall and straight. Place your right hand on the outer edge of

Continued...

ACTIVE

your left knee and your left hand on the base of your spine. Take a deep breath in as you are doing this, exhaling slowly. Once you have finished breathing out, switch over to the other side, with your left hand on the outer edge of your right knee and your right hand on the base on your spine.

Shoulder stretch – place your fingertips on the edge of your desk and push your chair back until your arms are straight, with your head in between your shoulders. Hold this position for at least 10 seconds, breathing deeply in and out as you do. Drop a pen on the floor first if you want to look as though you're trying to find something under your desk.

A LITTLE MORE OBVIOUS

Wrist release – reach your arms out directly in front of you, like a zombie, turn your hands over so that your palms are facing up and then bend your elbows so that your hands are directly in front of your face. Bend your wrists so that your fingertips are facing your shoulders. Then bend each wrist in the opposite direction, fingertips facing outwards. Next, turn your hands so that palms are facing and bend wrists so that fingertips are alternatively facing each other, then facing out. Finally, to fully release any other tension, stretch both arms out like a scarecrow and give your wrists a good rapid shake side to side.

CLEARLY DOING YOGA

Forward fold – push your chair away from your desk so that you have a good amount of space around you. With feet firmly on the ground, interlace your fingers behind your back. Slowly roll forward, lifting your arms as you go, until your chest is on your knees or as close as you can get. Hang your head between your knees and hold the position until you feel it is time to come up.

Alternatively, if you're really happy for your colleagues to know what you're doing, get rid of the chair altogether and stand next to your desk, feet slightly apart. Fold over in half (you can relax your knees) and let your arms hang down. Hold for at least 20 seconds and sway from side to side if desired. As well as realigning your neck and shoulders, this exercise will reverse the blood flow and give you the energizing boost needed for a productive afternoon.

ACTIVE

VISIT LOCAL STUDIOS OR WORKSHOPS

Inject a burst of creativity, colour and craftsmanship into your lunch breaks this week!

1 Minimum lunch breaks needed

25 Minimum time needed (mins) + journey time

LUNCH BREAKS TAKEN

RATING OUT OF 10

ENERGY OUT OF 10

Surrounded by computer screens, monochrome office workers and a nine-to-five mentality, it's easy to assume that everyone around you is in the same situation. The creative heart of a city usually feels miles away from its corporate core, but you'd be surprised by how many artists and makers have their studio spaces within walking distance of your office.

You might have to do a bit of digging to find these places. A lot of studios won't have websites, and they will often be discreetly tucked away under railway arches, in business parks or unoccupied office blocks. Try a simple internet search, to see if anything comes up and then, if not, use the "Nearby" search option in Google Maps. This is a godsend in helping you discover what's just around the corner and often turns up a multitude of hidden treasures. Use the search terms "studio", "workshop", "craft", "artist" and "maker".

Some cities also have "Open Studio" weeks or weekends, with online resources listing nearby private studios that usually aren't open to the public. If you discover one near your workplace, don't be scared to email the artist or maker and ask if you can visit one lunchtime. They will most likely be delighted to learn of your interest and will welcome you with open arms!

STUDIOS YOU HAVE VISITED THIS WEEK

VOLUNTEERING

Share your lunch break this week with someone in need of company, advice or just an extra pair of hands.

LUNCH BREAKS TAKEN

ENERGY
OUT OF 10

RATING
OUT OF 10

1 Minimum lunch breaks needed

45 Minimum time needed (mins) + journey time

Unless you live within walking distance of your workplace, it's easy to feel detached from the local community around your office. Get actively involved and offer your services to a nearby charity or hospital. The experience will be an uplifting one, broadening your weekday horizons and, in particular, putting any personal work stresses into perspective.

There are lots of different ways to volunteer during a lunch break. You could help out at a local homeless shelter or soup kitchen, serving lunch or washing up dishes. If you prefer something a little calmer, you could visit someone with no friends or family in hospital, or take lunch round to an elderly or housebound person. Go online to search for volunteering opportunities near your office, or contact your nearest shelter, church or hospital.

However you choose to volunteer, make sure you go through a registered charity or public body, and that there are appropriate support systems in place, in case of emergencies.

Where	What you did	Who you met

MAKE A MINI-DOCUMENTARY

With the amazing quality of smartphone cameras and the wealth of film editing apps that can be downloaded from app stores, anyone can be a budding Michael Moore these days.

 5 Minimum lunch breaks needed

 40 Minimum time needed (mins)

 LUNCH BREAKS TAKEN

RATING OUT OF 10

 ENERGY OUT OF 10

It takes a lot of time to create a full-blown documentary, so aim for just a 5-minute mini-documentary this week. You will need as many lunch breaks as you can manage, as the full process will include planning, scripting, filming and editing your documentary.

Think about the subject or theme of your production.

Bear in mind that the heavier or more complex the topic, the more filming and editing you will need to do. Some of the best documentaries are the simplest ones, with the narrowest focus.

Watch the first 5 minutes of a few documentaries online for some inspiration, preferably each by a different production company.

Notice the different styles: is there a presenter, or just a voiceover? Does the presenter talk to the camera, or are they in conversation with someone else? Are there lots of images shown in quick succession, or does the camera stay focused on a single subject, or a view, for a long time? Identify which approach you like best and think about how you can make it work with your chosen subject. Then, once you have this in mind, follow the steps coming up to make sure you come out with the most engaging production possible.

DON'T FORGET
To make sure you have enough memory and battery on your phone before you start filming.

Identify a question – once you have chosen your subject, work out why it fascinates you. What do you want to learn about it by the end of the documentary? What might a viewer who has no previous knowledge of the subject whatsoever need to know about it?

Make it personal – don't spend too much time worrying about what the audience will think. If you

ACTIVE

Continued...

love it, they'll love it. If you're laughing or crying while filming, there's a chance this is how they will respond as well. You are the primary audience member; the others will follow.

Plan your beginning, middle and end – work out how you will introduce the documentary and tell the viewer what it is about. Next, use as much content as you can to support the argument you set out in the introduction; this could also include counter-arguments. Finally, how will you conclude your documentary? Will you answer the question you posed or leave the viewer to decide? Write down your plan, including a list of images and footage you will need for each section, and a series of questions that you want to answer during the course of the documentary. Divide it into days, so you know what you need to accomplish each lunchtime. Leave at least one lunch break for the editing process.

Sound is as important as image – there's nothing worse than watching a documentary and all you can hear is the traffic in the background. Record your sound separately, if needed, and lay it over the footage afterwards. This could be done at home in the evenings. Bathrooms always have great acoustics.

Less is more – be concise, direct and don't over-complicate things – either visually or verbally.

Ask for permission – if you're filming strangers, or images that might be under copyright, make sure you ask the individual, publisher or gallery first. Tell them it is for a small-scale, personal project, although if you are planning to upload it to a website once finished, you might need to mention that it will be shared online.

WRITE DOWN IDEAS FOR YOUR MINI-DOCUMENTARY HERE

INSIDE

LUNCH-TIME CONCERTS

In most cities and towns, the local churches, universities or colleges often offer free lunchtime concerts during the weekdays.

1 Minimum lunch breaks needed

20 Minimum time needed (mins) + journey time

 LUNCH BREAKS TAKEN

 ENERGY OUT OF 10

 RATING OUT OF 10

The concerts are usually programmed with workers in mind and they will never last longer than 30–40 minutes. They will also be set up so that you can drop in and out, depending on how much time you have.

Don't panic if you don't feel you can commit to a whole concert. Even 10 or 20 minutes will be more than enough to transport you to another world and, if you like it, you can always go back for more another day.

You might have to do a bit of digging around to find your nearest lunchtime concert – churches in particular don't always have websites and may just advertise their concerts on a board outside their entrance. If you're struggling to find details online, walk past a couple of potential venues on your way to or from work and see if you can find anything out in person.

If you don't work near any lunchtime concert venues, national radio stations will often have similar programmes and sometimes live recordings of lunchtime concerts. You could also try streaming or downloading music you've never listened to before. (See **LISTEN TO AN ENTIRE BALLET OR OPERA** on page 28.) However you source the

music, find somewhere peaceful to sit – away from your desk – while listening: a park, a museum or gallery, or just a very comfortable sofa in a nearby café.

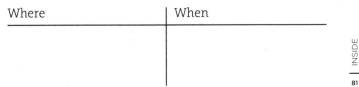

DON'T FORGET
There is so much music in the world, and so many different genres! If your first lunchtime concert doesn't quite hit the nail on the head, don't give up. Try another venue, or go back another day or week. Programmes and musicians change and it will be hard to get it right every time.

FIND YOUR NEAREST CONCERTS

Where	When

LUNCH WITH COLLEAGUES

Colleagues: you spend your whole working day with them, not to mention training days, away days, bonding days and even some evenings and weekends. And then there's the Christmas party. Do you really have to spend lunch breaks together too?

1	Minimum lunch breaks needed
40	Minimum time needed (mins)

LUNCH BREAKS TAKEN

RATING OUT OF 10

ENERGY OUT OF 10

Sometimes we slip into viewing our office-mates purely in terms of work. We consider their levels of efficiency, we quietly watch how many hours they do and we judge them on their professionalism. This is all fair enough – you're there to do a job after all – but, bearing in mind that you spend the majority of your waking week with your colleagues, how well do you know them, just as people?

Try to go for lunch with as many colleagues as possible this week. Start with the ones you know and then, if you're feeling confident enough, invite a few who you don't know so well. You can always start your email with "Sounds mad, but I've bought this book about doing things with my lunch break and…"

You'll be surprised by how refreshing these lunches will be and how much of a mental break from work they provide, even though, physically, you're with the same people and possibly in the same space as the rest of your working day. They are also a great bonding experience, because you will both feel like you have helped each other escape a little. It's a bit like sharing a secret.

SOME CONVERSATION TOPICS TO GET YOU STARTED

- **Their local area** – where do they live; what's it like at the weekends?
- **Books** – ask for a recommendation, or what their favourite book is.

- **Music** – have they been to any good gigs or concerts lately?
- **Holidays** – have they just been on one or do they have any planned? What's been their favourite holiday?

BOOKSHOP
BROWSING*

With all the ease and speed
of downloading or ordering
books online, spending time
browsing in bookshops
is a dying pastime.

**LUNCH
BREAKS
TAKEN**

ENERGY
OUT OF 10

RATING
OUT OF 10

1 Minimum lunch
breaks needed

30 Minimum time
needed (mins)
+ journey time

Not only does this mean
limited opportunities
to chance upon the best
book you've never read
but, mentally and
physically, it deprives us
of a great deal of peace
and contemplation.

When browsing in a
bookshop, you'll find that
you enter a state close to
dreaming. Your immediate
physical sensations will
become muted as you

dive in and out of a host
of different loves, lives,
adventures and discoveries.

Everyone has their own
preferred method of
browsing, but in case
you're new to the idea,
here are a few tips.

TIPS FOR BROWSING

1. Choose a genre that
   interests you already:
   Fiction, Biography,
   History, Design.

2. Judge books by their covers – go for the one that jumps out at you.

3. Ease yourself in gently:
– Read the first line. If you like it...
– Read the second line. If you like it...
– Read the first ten lines. If you like them...
– Read the first page and a half. If you're still going after three or four pages...
– Buy the book (sounds silly, but many books dwindle after the third paragraph).

4. If you're not sure you want to buy the book straight away, take a photo or write down the title.

* Try to do this challenge before the **READ A BOOK YOU'VE ALWAYS MEANT TO** challenge on page 22.

DON'T FORGET
To keep an eye on the time. You'll be amazed by how quickly books can swallow it.

BOOKS YOU LIKED

Author	Title

LOCAL CAFÉS, PUBS AND RESTAURANTS

How many times in your working week do you use the phrase "grab a sandwich"? Every day?

1 Minimum lunch breaks needed

30 Minimum time needed (mins) + journey time

 LUNCH BREAKS TAKEN

 RATING OUT OF 10

ENERGY OUT OF 10

Lunch as a meal, in the sit-down, sociable sense of the word, has almost ceased to exist during the working week. Instead, it's become a refuelling process – something you leave off until your hunger won't be ignored any longer.

Nine times out of ten, you probably head for the nearest supermarket or chain café. We love them for their familiarity: no matter where we are, they will always look the same. We love the predictable, smiling staff. We love the un-changing menus, so that we know exactly what we're getting before we've even entered the building. In fact, choosing what to eat on the spot in a chain café is probably one of the more stressful lunchtime experiences.

Reacquaint yourself with lunch as a meal this week, and opt not to take away, but to eat in.

Local, independent cafés, pubs and restaurants are the best places to go to, mainly because they are set up with eaters-in, rather than "grabbers", in mind. They are also often family run, so have a welcoming and warm atmosphere, and the menus are usually much more creative and finely tuned to the chef's skills. And they're not as expensive as you'd expect.

Do some research, read some reviews and find the best local eateries near you. Try to be a bit chatty when you're in there too, if the opportunity presents itself. Remember: meals are supposed to be social occasions.

Where you went	What you ate

GO ON A DATE

Forget candlelit dinners and long, awkward cocktail-fuelled conversations that you want to finish as soon as they've started.

1   Minimum lunch breaks needed

40   Minimum time needed (mins) + journey time

LUNCH BREAKS TAKEN

ENERGY OUT OF 10

RATING OUT OF 10

Studies have shown that we only need one-tenth of a second to form an initial judgment of another person, and 3 minutes to decide if we are attracted to them or not!

Lunch breaks seem almost too good an opportunity to miss for a first date. The short time allowance means you can keep things casual; there will rarely be any awkwardness about who pays the bill; if it's all going horribly wrong you can make a show of looking at the time, gasping and apologizing for having to get back to work for a meeting; and it leaves your evenings and weekends free to spend with people you actually want to see.

And if it all goes right, you can whip the candles out for the second date another evening. What are you waiting for?

Online dating sites and apps are the best resources for setting up your dates, as you will be able to search by location and find the best eligible singles near your office. Some websites are set up with lunchtime dating specifically in mind, so have a look online and see if there is anything near you, otherwise the big, nationwide dating services shouldn't let you down.

DON'T FORGET
Avoid date venues too close to your office. There's nothing worse than bumping into your boss while on a date and potentially having to introduce your companion.

You met	What you liked about them	Second date?

TAKE A GAMBLE

Before the days of 24-hour casinos and betting apps, the idea of gambling was traditionally linked to the perception that every creature in the world is subject to chance and, regardless of how much we try to plan and control things, the unexpected can always happen.

1 Minimum lunch breaks needed

30 Minimum time needed (mins)

LUNCH BREAKS TAKEN

RATING OUT OF 10

ENERGY OUT OF 10

In gambling, the human intellect is pitched against the unpredictable forces of fate or fortune. When we consciously gamble, we are participating in a concentrated form of the risk-taking behaviour we carry out every day. Gambling tests our judgement and challenges our prudence in terms of how much we are prepared to lose and whether we know when to walk away with our winnings, or to cut our losses and stop playing before we get carried away. As an activity, it trains the mind to handle risk and enhances the skills needed when weighing up more calculating ventures, especially in business. It also reminds us that the wheel of fortune is ever turning and to beware the individual who thinks they are on a permanent winning streak!

Find a partner to surrender yourself to the fates with and take a chance on a game of cards this week. Poker, Bridge and Gin Rummy are three of the best and most popular games to stake your fortunes on. However, to keep things light (and safe), don't go for a financial gamble. Use counters, matchsticks, paper-clips or small change. The purpose of this activity is to test your judgement and your risk-taking abilities, not to clear out your bank account.

DON'T FORGET
To quit while you're ahead.

Game	Opponent	Score

LUNCHTIME TALKS

Broaden your horizons, challenge your perceptions and thrash out some ideas this week by attending or listening to some lunchtime talks.

LUNCH
BREAKS
TAKEN

ENERGY
OUT OF 10

RATING
OUT OF 10

 1 Minimum lunch breaks needed

30 Minimum time needed (mins) + journey time

Similar to lunchtime concerts and lunchtime theatre, a lot of venues – especially universities, colleges and cultural institutions – have a programme of midday talks that are designed to fit perfectly within the time constraints of a working lunch.

Search online for your nearest lunchtime talk, take a sandwich along with you and listen to some big ideas as they are explained, explored and discussed. If there are no venues within walking distance of your workplace, try national radio stations or podcasts as a moveable alternative (see **LISTEN TO A PODCAST** on page 54).

If none of these options are possible, you could always set up a programme of lunchtime talks at your workplace – inviting different speakers in and asking colleagues to join for a "lunch and learn".

TALKS YOU HAVE LISTENED TO THIS WEEK

Speaker	Topic

LUNCHTIME THEATRE

There is a strange distinction between going to the theatre and going to the cinema. While you will often leave the cinema feeling a mixture of sleepy and a little fidgety, going to the theatre is always an energizing experience.

 1 Minimum lunch breaks needed

40 Minimum time needed (mins) + journey time

LUNCH BREAKS TAKEN

RATING OUT OF 10

ENERGY OUT OF 10

There's something electrifying about watching a live performance; we feel inspired and enlightened, having formed a close connection with both the actors and the script, which occasionally – if we really love it – we will go away and read afterwards. While a film primarily provides a visual stimulation, a theatrical production offers an intellectual one; our brain engages with the two media in a different way.

Concerned about the aging demographic of their audiences, many theatres are trying to make attending plays more accessible for people who might not have the time, or money, to frequent them in the usual way.

DON'T FORGET
To turn your phone off during the performance.

As a result, a growing number of theatres are now offering short, lunchtime productions for local workers to attend. The plays usually last no longer than 40 minutes and will include an alluring ticket offer, e.g. lunch or a drink will be included.

Go online to see if there are any lunchtime performances taking place near your office. As this is a fairly new initiative for many theatres, and the word hasn't reached a large audience yet, it's unlikely that you will find a theatre that offers lunchtime plays every week. You will probably have to plan this activity in advance, possibly even by a few months, in order to catch a suitable production nearby.

As ever, if there's no information available online, contact your local theatre and ask if they have any intention of programming lunchtime plays in the near future. Universities and drama schools are also good places to look but, again, the performances will be infrequent.

PRODUCTIONS YOU HAVE SEEN THIS WEEK

PLAN
A MEAL

At the end a long
day, it's all too
tempting (and
easy) to reach for
the nearest ready
meal or takeaway
menu and spend the
evening vegging out
in front of the TV.

1 Minimum lunch
breaks needed

30 Minimum time
needed (mins)

**LUNCH
BREAKS
TAKEN**

ENERGY
OUT OF 10

RATING
OUT OF 10

After at least eight hours
of work, we don't always
feel like we have the
mental or physical energy
to plan and cook an entire
meal from scratch.

Shift the planning to
earlier in the day, though,
and the excitement and
anticipation about the
meal you have designed
will propel you well into
the evening, leaving you
healthier and happier by
the time you go to sleep.

Don't just use your
lunch break to decide
that you'll be cooking
your favourite pasta
dish again; force
yourself to learn a new
recipe or to try a new
way of cooking. The
easiest way to do this
is to base your meal
around an ingredient
that you're not used
to cooking with. This
could be a type of fish,

meat, seafood, cheese or seasonal vegetable.

If you work near a wholefood or farmer's market, these are great places to go and discover new and interesting produce, as it will always be seasonal. The stallholders usually have expert knowledge about their produce, too, so they will be able to give you advice on the best way to prepare and cook it, or the tastiest ingredients to pair it with.

If you're not near a market, ask your colleagues or friends for their favourite recipes. Try to make this a personal culinary experiment, incorporating tips and flavours contributed by the people you are closest to. Whatever recipe you end up choosing, make sure you don't just sit

at your desk trawling through the internet for ideas. Get out and have a good look at the food you'll be cooking. This activity is about colour, taste, touch and smell, not clicking and scrolling.

DON'T FORGET
Choose your products based on when they are in season. They will taste all the better for it.

MEALS PLANNED

HAVE A POWER NAP

"I'm just going for a quick nap" isn't something you'd be chomping at the bit to tell your boss on the busiest day of the year. But power naps might be one of the most efficient ways of recharging your brain in the middle of the day and optimizing your levels of concentration, energy and creativity.

1 Minimum lunch breaks needed

10 Minimum time needed (mins)

LUNCH BREAKS TAKEN

RATING OUT OF 10

ENERGY OUT OF 10

A power nap is a short sleep lasting between 10 and 30 minutes, ideally taken at some point before 4PM. Any later than this and you run the risk of disrupting your regular night-time sleep patterns. Likewise, make sure you don't go over 30 minutes – not only for your career's sake but also because the longer you sleep, the deeper you go and the harder it is to pull yourself out of it.

The benefits of power napping are near to endless. It decreases everything that's bad (stress, tension, depression, fatigue) and increases everything that's good, from alertness, creativity and productivity, to memory, learning, problem solving and reasoning. On top of all this, it's beneficial for your heart, blood pressure and, surprisingly, weight management.

One study showed how naps help compensate for "sleep deficits" – those occasional midnight hours when you wake up and just can't get back to sleep. This helps to steady our metabolism and hormone levels, so that our bodies can process carbohydrates properly. That and, if you're a napper, you're less likely to turn to high-energy (high-sugar) drinks or large, milky cups of sweetened coffee – both of which would hit the hips pretty quickly.

Find a comfortable, private place where you can switch off for 10 minutes. Your office might have some armchairs or a sofa you could curl up on, or find a café with a cosy seat in the corner. People will know you're power napping, so don't worry about looking weird; just concentrate on recharging.

DON'T FORGET
To set an alarm.

LUNCHTIME CHOIR

If you're fed up of speaking in polite, professional and muted tones across an open-plan office, let your voice ring loud this week and join a lunchtime choir for a good old sing-a-long.

LUNCH BREAKS TAKEN

ENERGY
OUT OF 10

RATING
OUT OF 10

1 Minimum lunch breaks needed

45 Minimum time needed (mins) + journey time

The benefits of singing are almost endless. Not only does bursting into song exercise your lungs and develop healthier breathing patterns, it is also a full-blown aerobic activity that exercises major muscle groups in the upper body, even when sitting.

On top of its tonal advantages, when you sing, you release endorphins, your body's homemade feel-good stimulator, as well as oxytocin, a natural stress reliever that has been found to alleviate feelings of depression and loneliness. Not to mention the increased sense of community, belonging and shared endeavour that being part of a choir engenders.

Search online for your nearest lunchtime choir. If you can't find anything straight away, you might have to drop into churches, universities, libraries or community centres to see if there is anything advertised on their notice boards. If nothing exists, think about starting one up – post an ad online and see if anyone responds.

If you are based in a rural location and there are no choirs, or potential choirs, to be found, take your headphones for a walk to a remote place, press play, and sing your heart out to the hills (and pray that nobody's passing nearby).

DON'T FORGET
You don't have to be pitch perfect to reap the benefits of singing. If it's a lunchtime choir that you're joining, most of your fellow singers will be amateurs who are also looking to fit singing into their day without seriously devoting evenings and weekends to it. Join in for the joy of it.

SONGS YOU HAVE SUNG THIS WEEK

PRAY, WISH, HOPE

Prayer: an earnest hope or wish.

1 Minimum lunch breaks needed

10 Minimum time needed (mins) + journey time

LUNCH BREAKS TAKEN

RATING OUT OF 10

ENERGY OUT OF 10

As a religious practice, prayer can be a slightly foreign or uncomfortable topic for a lot of people. However, as a mindful endeavour, there is no reason why it should only be an activity for the religious.

Similar to meditation, praying reduces stress, increases focus and concentration, and helps us gain some perspective on our worries and fears. However, where prayer differs to meditation is that it encourages us to

focus less on ourselves, and more on other people. While self-reflection is no bad thing, it can mean that we run the risk of losing some perspective on our fortunes and misfortunes, in relation to other people.

To pray, in this context, means to spend some time thinking about those you care about and internally wishing the best for them. You don't need to be in a religious building, and you don't need to address your prayer to a higher being; just spend some time contemplating in a quiet place and, when you're ready, mentally think out loud a few sentences beginning with "I hope..." or "I wish..."

It is not a wasted exercise. It will make you more aware of those closest to you, which will affect the way you interact with them. It might remind you of someone you haven't spoken to for a while and prompt you to get back in touch with them. It will remind you of the principles you uphold and the values or qualities in life that you believe to be important. And, in terms of personal benefit, it will make many of your own troubles feel relatively equal, if not smaller, to other people's.

DON'T FORGET
Don't be scared by the idea of praying! At its most simple level, it is just thinking about other people.

Who did you think about?	What did you hope for?

TREAT YOURSELF

As many skyscrapers as there are to climb, languages to learn and bicycle rides to embark on, we all have days when we just want to be a bit self-indulgent.

1 Minimum lunch breaks needed

30 Minimum time needed (mins)

LUNCH BREAKS TAKEN

RATING OUT OF 10

ENERGY OUT OF 10

Spending your lunch break clothes shopping, or getting a massage, haircut, manicure or pedicure, does not equate to laziness or selfishness. "Self-care", as this activity is kindly called, is incredibly important for your health and stress management. By taking time out, you are saving yourself from becoming physically or emotionally drained. This means that, when unexpected stresses come your way, you're able to deal with them head on. In other words, treating yourself to a little pampering every now and then will actually make you more mentally resilient.

There are physical benefits to occasional self-love too. Sitting hunched in front of a computer all day creates a lot of tension in your neck, back and shoulders.

Massages can help release this tension, along with reducing anxiety, digestive disorders and headaches. Likewise, going for a facial or a body scrub can help you detox by releasing toxins.

And if a rub down isn't your thing, a simple shopping trip for some new clothes, a haircut or a manicure will lift your spirits, give you a sense of renewal and leave you walking back to the office feeling brighter, lighter and more optimistic – and looking amazing.

DON'T FORGET
To banish your mother's/father's voice in your head. It's not a waste of money and it's only for a week.

YOUR FAVOURITE TREATS

OUTSIDE

GREEN SPACES

Going to sit in a park on a sunny day is hardly a groundbreaking idea, but when did you actually last do this during a working lunch?

1 Minimum lunch breaks needed

10 Minimum time needed (mins) + journey time

 LUNCH BREAKS TAKEN

 ENERGY OUT OF 10

 RATING OUT OF 10

It's not just about getting out of the office. Studies have shown that spending as little as 40 seconds looking out over some living, green space can seriously boost concentration. Even better, exposure to nature contributes to physical wellbeing, reducing blood pressure, heart rate, muscle tension, and the production of stress hormones. Rather sadly, apparently the introduction of just a single plant into an office space has a proven impact on improving employee stress and anxiety levels. Our bodies need green.

With the single plant in mind, even if your office is miles away from the nearest park, any type of green space will do: a small garden, a roof terrace, a living wall, a bench beneath a tree.

Just 10 minutes will be enough to calm you down, let you breathe and get some perspective on work-related stresses. Although, as with anything that involves relaxing, the longer you can take over it, the better.

DON'T FORGET
It needs to be green.

YOUR NEAREST GREEN SPACES

WATERWAYS

If you're having a week of information overload, ponds, rivers and fountains should provide you with a refreshing burst of tranquility.

1 Minimum lunch breaks needed

15 Minimum time needed (mins) + journey time

LUNCH BREAKS TAKEN

RATING OUT OF 10

ENERGY OUT OF 10

The many therapeutic qualities of direct, physical involvement with water are readily acknowledged – drinking mineral water, going to a thermal bath or taking a swim in a mountain lake are all fabled to improve your health.

Recent research has shown how important merely looking at water is, especially for our brains. When we look at water, compared to crowds of people, busy cityscapes or computer screens full of emails and spreadsheets, our brains can relax because there is less information to process. We enter an almost meditative state, our minds focused yet calm.

This in turn allows us to wonder, to imagine, to reflect and to create. Supposedly this is why many people suddenly come up with solutions to problems when in the shower or bath. Maybe your next team meeting should be near a waterway...

Go online to look at a map of your local area and see where your nearest waterway is. Remember that you want to be able to sit in relative peace next to the water when you get there, so make sure it's not by the side of a road or in the middle of an industrial estate. Parks or river banks are usually the best places to perch. Keep in mind that this

challenge is about looking at the water, not just being near it. Try to keep your eye focused on the water's surface for as long as possible, so that your brain can get the downtime it needs and you can return to the office feeling like you've had a fullblown dip.

DON'T FORGET
A notebook. That eureka moment is just around the river bend.

YOUR NEAREST WATERWAYS

DRAW A BUILDING*

How do you view the built environment around your office? Are you in the middle of a concrete jungle, surrounded by glass and steel sheets that reflect the grey pavements and cast long shadows along the streets? Or are you inspired by classical arcades, gothic spires and Art Deco elevations?

 1 Minimum lunch breaks needed

30 Minimum time needed (mins)

 LUNCH BREAKS TAKEN

 RATING OUT OF 10

 ENERGY OUT OF 10

Whatever your relationship with the buildings around you, shake things up this week by paying them a bit more attention than usual.

Take a pad of paper, a pen or a pencil and draw a building that you are moved, disgusted or intrigued by. You'll find that your feelings about

architecture in general will change over the course of the week.

As with all drawing-related challenges, the break from words and linear thought will give your brain some much needed down-time in the middle of the day. The modular and often predictable shapes of buildings also mean that you don't have to keep looking up but can focus on the page for longer, going into an almost trance-like or meditative state while filling in repeated windows and doorways. Perfect for days when you're in need of something a little soothing, with minimal thinking required.

* There are a few different drawing challenges in this book. If you want something more anthropomorphic, with softer lines and a human subject, turn to page 18 for **DRAW A PORTRAIT**. If you want to switch off entirely, focusing only on the page without having to look up, turn to page 26 for **DOODLE**.

DON'T FORGET
Buildings may look like a series of squares and circles, but they often take much longer to draw than expected. If you're aiming to draw an entire cityscape, pace yourself and be aware that you might need several lunch breaks to finish it all.

PUBLIC ART

In comparison to blockbuster exhibitions at big-name galleries, public art is often quite heavily underappreciated.

LUNCH BREAKS TAKEN

ENERGY OUT OF 10

RATING OUT OF 10

1 Minimum lunch breaks needed

30 Minimum time needed (mins) + journey time

We walk past it on the way to and from the station or the sandwich shop, vaguely aware that it's there, but we rarely stop to consider it as actual art and, instead, think of it more as municipal decoration.

But noticing public art will transform the way you feel about the streets, squares and parks around your workplace. It will change alleyways and subways into corridors, leading you through an open-air exhibition of huge-scale works that you can walk around, touch, lean against and sit on.

Focusing on contemporary art this week – whether it's sculpture, installation or graffiti – spend a couple of lunch breaks researching the public art near your office and then go and view the pieces with your new-found knowledge in tow. If you'd rather look before you learn, go for a walk around, identify some works that intrigue you and research them only afterwards.

Art is always more fun when discussed in conversation, so if you want some company, invite a colleague or two along with you and give them a mini art tour, or just ask them for their opinions on what you're looking at. If you'd rather be on your own, use this time to enjoy the openness of the surrounding spaces and the fact that, unlike in a gallery, nobody is watching you look at the art, which should take the pressure off slightly!

DON'T FORGET
If you can't find any information about the artworks, you can still look at them. Public art is usually commissioned for specific spaces, to respond to environments or local histories and to encourage a greater connection with the public. Think about how the artworks transform, alter or respond to the surrounding area. Notice colour, form and material. Are they sympathetic or contrary to the nearby buildings? Do you like it or loathe it? Why?

ART AND ARTISTS YOU HAVE DISCOVERED THIS WEEK

TAKE A CAREFULLY CONSIDERED PHOTOGRAPH

With the modern wonder of camera-phones, we are all completely snap-happy these days.

1 Minimum lunch breaks needed

15 Minimum time needed (mins) + journey time

LUNCH BREAKS TAKEN

RATING OUT OF 10

ENERGY OUT OF 10

While this is great because it means even more of our memories can be instantly captured, without having to change the film or wind it on, it probably also means we think less about how or what we are photographing.

Take some time this week to be a bit more considered about the colour, form, subject and composition of your photographs.

If you can, spend a fair bit of time walking around looking for an interesting subject matter. Then, when you feel that you're ready to start snapping, consider some of the following handy tricks to make your photo its absolute best.

Turn gridlines on – this not only allows you to align any vertical and horizontal lines, but also to structure your image by dividing it into thirds, making it more visually pleasing and engaging.

Focus on a single subject – even if there is a lot going on in the background, make sure you highlight exactly what it is that's caught your eye. You can do this through composition (placing the subject at the centre or in front of everything else) or by manually focusing on the subject and making it sharper than the rest of the image.

Lead the eye into the photo – if your subject is a little obscure, look to see if there are any lines that can lead the viewer's eye straight towards what

you're looking at. This could be a path, a road, the edge of a building or a staircase: anything that carries the eye from one part of the photo to another.

Look for symmetry – one of the easiest ways to create a visually pleasing photo is to make it balanced. Use your gridlines to make sure everything is equally spaced and that lines are straight.

Use reflection – look for opportunities to play with reflection. Think about puddles, ponds, lakes, mirrors, sunglasses, glass and metallic surfaces.

Create a pattern – patterns are always satisfying, especially if you identify them

Continued...

in a subject that you'd otherwise think of as mundane. You might find a ready-made pattern in a textile or a natural material, or if you find several objects of interest, arrange them in a repetitive form to create an arresting image.

Don't zoom – even if you're far away. This will jeopardize the quality of the photo. It's much better to crop afterwards.

Turn the flash off – if you're taking this picture on your phone, it's unlikely that a flash will make it look better. Download a photo-editing app and alter light levels afterwards.

**PRINT OUT AND STICK A COPY OF
YOUR BEST PHOTOGRAPH HERE**

GARDENING

Gardening is one of the most natural and rewarding therapies around. You're outside, in the fresh air, surrounded by beautiful plants and intoxicating smells.

 1 Minimum lunch breaks needed

30 Minimum time needed (mins) + journey time

 LUNCH BREAKS TAKEN

RATING OUT OF 10

 ENERGY OUT OF 10

There's something innately soothing about getting green-fingered and working with living plants, especially when the only things your fingers have touched all day are keypads and touch-screens. The mental reassurance, too, of putting down seeds and watching them grow is a poignant and comforting reminder that things need time to develop – especially in our careers and personal lives.

In a more immediate way, recent research has found that, in a group of people who worked all day but stopped halfway through to take just a half-hour gardening break, their levels of the stress hormone cortisol were significantly lowered.

Gardening is also used to treat mental health issues and, if its benefits for the mind don't grab you, it's a great physical workout.

Find your nearest community or rooftop garden. Contact them and ask if you can offer half an hour a day for a week. If they feel this isn't enough time to get anything done, get a group of colleagues together and persuade the garden's owner that many hands make light work – even if it is just for 30 minutes a day!

If you can't find a garden near you, see if you could set something up at work. This could be as simple as creating a few plant boxes for the office windowsills, herb boxes for the staff kitchen or pots to go by the entrance. If you have roof space, think about planting a living roof of either grass or wild flowers. This will also help your company to offset their carbon footprint.

Living walls are also an option and can be fairly easy to create using an old wooden pallet turned on its side and attached to the wall. The slats make perfect, secure shelves for plant pots to be held in and if you choose hanging plants or creepers, they will soon cover the supporting structure. Get a team together and transform your office into a natural oasis. So much will improve...

DON'T FORGET
Wear gloves and wash your hands after you have finished.

STATUES OF IMPORTANT LOCAL FIGURES

Think of all the millions of people who, over the centuries, have walked the streets you walk down daily. What did they do, think and achieve?

1 Minimum lunch breaks needed

20 Minimum time needed (mins) + journey time

LUNCH BREAKS TAKEN

RATING OUT OF 10

ENERGY OUT OF 10

In any town or city, the world over, there will always be at least one pedestal-topping, skyward-gazing statue of an important individual. Depending on their level of historical fame, sometimes we know who they are, but often we're unaware of their identity or the reasoning behind them being placed where they are.

Learning about your local statues is a brilliant and personal way of discovering the history of the streets around your workplace and connecting you to the past. Rather than reading a broad, socio-political narrative in a book, you get to literally meet someone whose life story gives you a direct insight into the cultural and social nuances of their day. You also appreciate how their work has positively impacted on present-day society, shaped the city we live in and perhaps given us opportunities we might have otherwise not been entitled to.

Go for a walk around your office and see who you come across. Sometimes there will be full information on why they should be remembered; other times you will only be given their name, birth and death dates. If it's the latter, make a note of their name and go back and research them during your next lunch break. If their story is truly awe-inspiring, return to visit them another day, or spread the word about their good deeds and take a colleague on a short tour of your local statues.

Who is the statue of?	What did they do?

LOCAL WILDLIFE

Nature: how much interaction do you normally have with it during your working day? Do you even notice it? Contained in steely, spotless and air-conditioned offices, we can easily feel miles away from the natural world.

1 Minimum lunch breaks needed

20 Minimum time needed (mins) + journey time

LUNCH BREAKS TAKEN

ENERGY OUT OF 10

RATING OUT OF 10

But all around, above and beneath us – even in the middle of heaving cities – there are whole ecosystems of animals, birds and insects getting on with their daily existence: hunting, gathering, building, surviving. Looking for and contemplating these creatures can be an incredibly restorative experience. Seeing a bird soaring above you can have a similarly uplifting effect on your own mood; and there's something bizarrely reassuring about watching a small animal go about collecting food, or building a nest. It leaves you with the sense that everything and everyone has a purpose and, if you keep working and building, things will come to fruition.

From a physical and mental wellbeing point of view, this is another activity that makes you quiet and focused, close to meditative. Research has also shown that studying animals lowers the heart rate and blood pressure, and is a good way of reducing or relieving stress. It requires mental alertness, as often what you're looking for will come and go in the flash of an eye, and teaches us patience, usually followed by rich rewards.

Head to your nearest green space or waterway and see what you find. If you know the species but aren't sure of the breed you're looking at, make notes on the colours and markings of the creature and search online when you get back to the office.

Make a list of what you've seen and add drawings, if you're feeling Darwinian.

If you can't see anything straight away, listen for sounds like rustling leaves, or look for movement in trees. While helping you identify places where birds and animals might be, this also means that you will be blocking out all the other noise and confusion around you, providing some contemplative focus for your brain. If you don't live near a park or pond, look up!

DON'T FORGET
To be patient. It might take some time for these critters to emerge.

GHOST WALKS

Perfect for Halloween or a
dark, misty time of year...

1 Minimum lunch
breaks needed

45 Minimum time
needed (mins)

RATING
OUT OF 10

Every city has its ghosts. Some of these will be famous – you'll have heard stories about a ghostly garrison of Roman soldiers marching down the high street on the Ides of March – and some of them won't. For the sake of this challenge, you don't have to go on the hunt for actual sighted ghosts. You can include suspected ones.

Ghosts are usually representative of a trauma or a tragic occurrence that has emblazoned its memory on a local area. Find out a bit about sad and strange happenings near your workplace. Are there any gruesome murders, suspicious disappearances or tragic deaths?

Begin by trawling the internet for the history of your local area. If this doesn't produce any spooks, you could either try looking through books in your local library, or visiting your town's museum, although both of these are quite time intensive and still don't guarantee results. A much more fun and sociable way of finding out about your ghoulish neighbours is to think about the places where they might have lived or died – old buildings (dubious deaths), public squares (executions), pubs (brawls) – and then contact the person who either owns or is in charge of that space. Nine times out of ten, they'll have a story. If you're really lucky, there might even be a local ghost tour guide who can share some of their knowledge with you.

At the end of the week, if you've got a good menagerie of spectres, invite a couple of colleagues to join you as you walk around the streets and tell them tales that will make the hairs on the back of their necks stand up. A bit of a fright in the middle of the day is good for your heart...

DON'T FORGET
To scream.

YOUR LOCAL GHOSTS

Who	Where	Why they are haunting

GO FOR A WANDER

To wander: to go in a specified direction, typically slowly or by an indirect route.

1 Minimum lunch breaks needed

45 Minimum time needed (mins)

LUNCH BREAKS TAKEN

RATING OUT OF 10

ENERGY OUT OF 10

Going for a wander is not the same as going for a walk. Although "active", the main focus of wandering is on mental inquisitiveness, not physical exercise: your legs are only there to help your brain answer some questions. So if you've always wanted to know what's around the corner, or through that intriguing looking door, use your lunch break this week to go and find out!

Think about the areas around your office, in particular any streets that you've never been down before. If the thought of just setting off into the unknown is a little daunting, go online and have a look at a map of your local area. See if there's anything at the end of those uncharted streets that you'd like to aim for – a café, a park or a shop.

Plan your route, but not too much. Most importantly, don't stick to it and don't feel the need to actually reach your intended destination. The route-planning is just there to get you started. If you reach a fork in the road and the unplanned turning looks more interesting, take it. Now you're wandering...

Don't be scared of getting lost either. You'll never be too far away from a familiar landmark. Just remember that you need as much time to get back to your office as you do to get away from it, so start thinking about turning round after 20 minutes or so.

DON'T FORGET
To stop and look. Contradictory as it may sound, the joy of wandering is in the stopping as much as in the moving.

Where you went	What you discovered

ROOF TERRACES

In terms of sensations and responses, roof terraces are like a combination of **CLIMB TO THE HIGHEST POINT** (page 58) and **GREEN SPACES** (page 108).

 1 Minimum lunch breaks needed

30 Minimum time needed (mins) + journey time

LUNCH BREAKS TAKEN

RATING OUT OF 10

ENERGY OUT OF 10

They are elevating, calming and evocative. They can also offer a feeling of escape, or retreat, hidden from view and a secret to only those who know their whereabouts.

While there are no isolated mental or physical benefits to sitting on a terrace, the experience of walking out from a café or bar onto an unexpected roof garden is second to none, especially in a built-up area where it feels like a literal oasis. The sense of discovery, mixed with the surrounding tranquility, transports you miles away from the office, the busy streets and noisy traffic below.

Uncover the leafy paradises near your office this week and search for your nearest roof terraces. A lot of the time you will find these are part of hotels, bars or restaurants, so be prepared to pay for a potentially pricey coffee, but all-in-all the experience should be worth the investment, and the coffee will probably be really good, too.

DON'T
FORGET
To go back
to work.

YOUR NEAREST
ROOF TERRACES

VISIT A CEMETERY

Cemeteries and graveyards, contrary to their depiction in most Hollywood films, are usually places of peace and tranquility.

LUNCH BREAKS TAKEN

ENERGY
OUT OF 10

RATING
OUT OF 10

1 Minimum lunch breaks needed

20 Minimum time needed (mins) + journey time

They provide a space for silence, respect and contemplation, admittedly of mourning for some but also of comfort, as a touchstone with our ancestors.

They can also be areas of natural beauty, architectural intrigue and historical significance. Many cemeteries in large cities contain the tombs and resting places of famous or influential individuals, which sometimes become shrines or places of pilgrimage for people who share their ideas or appreciate the mark these individuals have left on the world.

Decide which approach you will take – the contemplative or the historically interested – and visit your nearest cemetery or graveyard. If you don't work near one of these, consider memorials, statues or even plaques on buildings and in parks and squares. Use this week as a time for quiet reflection, an opportunity to attain a little peace in the middle of a busy working day and a chance to learn.

FAMOUS GRAVES

Who	What they did

GRAPH YOUR
CHALLENGES

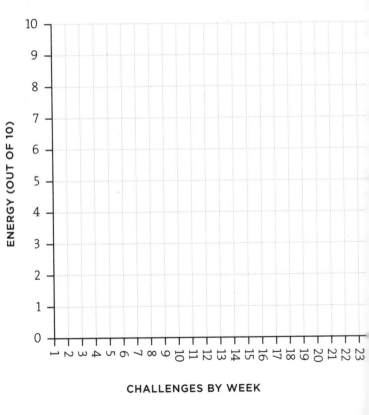

Plot your energy ratings for each week on this graph, listing the corresponding challenges on the pages overleaf. What was the most energizing way you spent your lunch break?

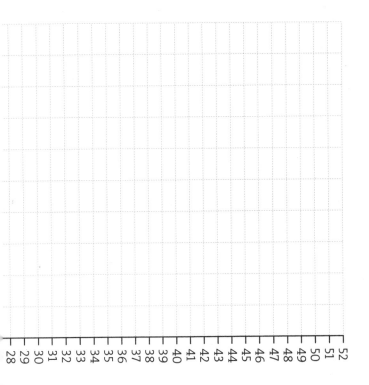

28 29 30 31 32 33 34 35 36 37 38 39 40 41 42 43 44 45 46 47 48 49 50 51 52

WHAT I DID THIS WEEK

Use this space to keep a record of how you spent your lunch breaks each week. Note down your favourite memories, places you've been, ideas, learnings, and things you want to come back to.

WEEK 1 (date: _____)

Challenge: _____

WEEK 2 (date: _____)

Challenge: _____

WEEK 3 (date: _____)

Challenge: _____

WEEK 4 (date: _____)

Challenge: _____

WEEK 5 (date: _____)

Challenge: _____

WEEK 6 (date: _____)

Challenge: _____

WEEK 7 (date: _____)

Challenge: _____

WEEK 8 (date: _____)

Challenge: _____

WEEK 9 (date: ___)

Challenge: _____

WEEK 10 (date: ___)

Challenge: _____

WEEK 11 (date: ___)

Challenge: _____

WEEK 12 (date: ___)

Challenge: _____

WEEK 13 (date: ___)

Challenge: _____

WEEK 14 (date: ___)

Challenge: _____

WEEK 15 (date: ___)

Challenge: _____

WEEK 16 (date: ___)

Challenge: _____

WEEK 17 (date: ___)

Challenge: _____

WEEK 18 (date: ___)

Challenge: _____

WEEK 19 (date: ___)

Challenge: _____

WEEK 20 (date: ___)

Challenge: _____

WEEK 21 (date: ___)

Challenge: _____

WEEK 22 (date: ___)

Challenge: _____

WEEK 23 (date: ___)

Challenge: _____

WEEK 24 (date: ___)

Challenge: _____

WEEK 25 (date: ____)

Challenge: _____

WEEK 26 (date: ____)

Challenge: _____

WEEK 27 (date: ____)

Challenge: _____

WEEK 28 (date: ____)

Challenge: _____

WEEK 29 (date: ____)

Challenge: _____

WEEK 30 (date: ____)

Challenge: _____

WEEK 31 (date: ____)

Challenge: _____

WEEK 32 (date: ____)

Challenge: _____

WEEK 33 (date: ___)

Challenge: _____

WEEK 34 (date: ___)

Challenge: _____

WEEK 35 (date: ___)

Challenge: _____

WEEK 36 (date: ___)

Challenge: _____

WEEK 37 (date: ___)

Challenge: _____

WEEK 38 (date: ___)

Challenge: _____

WEEK 39 (date: ___)

Challenge: _____

WEEK 40 (date: ___)

Challenge: _____

WEEK 41 (date: ____)
Challenge: _____

WEEK 42 (date:)
Challenge: _____

WEEK 43 (date:)
Challenge: _____

WEEK 44 (date:)
Challenge: _____

WEEK 45 (date: ____)
Challenge: _____

WEEK 46 (date:)
Challenge: _____

WEEK 47 (date:)
Challenge: _____

WEEK 48 (date:)
Challenge: _____

WEEK 49 (date: ____)

Challenge: _____

WEEK 50 (date:)

Challenge: _____

WEEK 51 (date:)

Challenge: _____

WEEK 52 (date:)

Challenge: _____

All my thanks go to my gorgeous family for their constant encouragement and support; my friends for their fascination, joy and wanderlust; my godmother Susie and her family for their guidance and advice; my cactus for his love at the beginning; and the Irelands for food, shelter and sea air while I wrote. Also to my agent Louise Lamont and my editor Céline Hughes, for such an exciting and stimulating few months bringing everything together. And finally to my employer and colleagues, for their support of lunch breaks!

Publishing director
Sarah Lavelle
Creative director Helen Lewis
Commissioning editor
Céline Hughes
Designer and illustrator
Emily Lapworth
Production Emily Noto,
Vincent Smith

First published in 2017 by
Quadrille Publishing
Pentagon House,
52–54 Southwark Street,
London SE1 1UN

Quadrille Publishing is an
imprint of Hardie Grant
www.hardiegrant.com.au
www.quadrille.co.uk
www.quadrille.com

Reprinted in 2017
10 9 8 7 6 5 4 3 2

Text © Laura Archer 2017

Design and layout
© 2017 Quadrille Publishing

Cataloguing in Publication Data:
a catalogue record for this
book is available from the
British Library.

ISBN: 978 184949 991 0

Printed in China